Drink Time!

friend,

I rather share
a drink and
a good talk
with - each
moment
in your
company
a
grace.

Let it
be a
good one.

♡-
Maya

Στη Rosa, τη μητέρα μου
εύχομαι μακροζωία

Drink Time!

In the Company of Patrick Leigh Fermor

A Memoir by Dolores Payás

TRANSLATED BY AMANDA HOKINSON

KR Publishing

Drink Time!

Published in 2016 by

KR Publishing

contact
www.dolorespayas.com

ISBN- 978-1530526680
Original © Dolores Payás
All photographs © Dolores Payás
English Translation © Amanda Hopkinson

Original tittle: *Drink Time! (en compañía de Patrick Leigh Fermor)*
First published in 2013 by Editorial Acantilado, Barcelona

Cover and book design by Nick Caya
Word-2-Kindle.com

The excerpts from
Roumeli - Travels in Northen Greece (© Patrick Leigh Fermor 1966) and *Mani
- Travels in Southern Greece* (© Patrick Leigh Fermor 1958) are reproduced by
kind permission of
John Murray Press, and imprint of Hodder
and Stoughton Limited

CONTENTS

Introduction

There are certain people who, without seeking or even wishing to do so, acquire an immense importance in the lives of others they touch. They are the men and women who reconfigure new worlds, create landscapes, conjure up horizons or redirect life along unforeseen paths.

Relationships with such individuals are rarely evenly balanced but this need not imply any offence to either party involved. Anyone with the good fortune to have come within their orbit learns how impossible it is to respond to them in an even-handed manner. For these individuals, men and women alike, are walking treasures. Their personalities emanate a rich charisma that extends well beyond what might normally be expected. Or else they exercise the kind of influence on their circle that well exceeds that of any ordinary artist.

Patrick Leigh Fermor was one such individual.

I knew him when he was already well advanced in years. He could scarcely see and had considerable difficulty in hearing.

Without a doubt, my appearance was little more than a fleeting and hazy shade at the end of his days. In contrast, the mark he himself left was profound and enduring.

What follows is an unabashed homage. A homage to the adventurer and author, to the gentleman and jovial host, and to the intrepid warrior. The person who knew how to transform himself into an invincible elderly man, proud and adorable, while retaining every one of the afore-mentioned attributes.

This text lays no claim to be exhaustive or biographical. It is merely intended as an affectionate portrait: a sketch inspired by informal chats, dinners, whole evenings and an impressive quantity of wine drunk together. Most of all, it is intended to evoke the stays at the home of this author in the weeks before his death.

Readers who are as yet unaware of the life of Leigh Fermor would do well to consult the biographical appendix before starting to read this book from the beginning. They will then enjoy the ensuing pages all the more, having once familiarised themselves with the brief account of the author's adventures.

It will come as no surprise that Sir Patrick Leigh Fermor is almost invariably referred to with the simple familiarity inherent in the nickname Paddy. That was the name his friends and acquaintances knew him by, as did indeed the literary media. In Greece he was more usually known as *o Mihalis*, but thereby hangs another tale...

Καρδαμύλη
(Kardamili)

Cooled in summer by the breeze from the gulf, the
great screen of the Taygetus shuts out intruding winds
from the north and the east; no tramontana can reach it.
It is like those Elysian confines of the world where Homer
says that life is easiest for men; where no snow falls,
no strong winds blow nor rain comes down, but
the melodious west wind blows for ever from
the sea to bring coolness to those who
live there. I was very much
tempted to become one
of them...
MANI

The route to Kardamili is a treacherous one. "Very deceptive" as Paddy used to say, working hard to pinpoint the right adjective, which to a Spanish listener possesses a sonority with hints of disappointment (even while this is not its literal meaning[1]). That's for sure. After passing over the Corinth Canal, one has to cross the Peloponnese from one end to the other. It is a demanding journey[2]. Bare, dark mountains, sharp escarpments, sheer descents; long hours of bends and menacing lorries. At length you reach Kalamata on the opposite coast. Kardamili lies at the edge of the ocean, a few kilometres further south, and natural logic would dictate a better route might be to get there by venturing along the coast. Instead the reverse turns out to be the case. The road switches back to meet the sky and returns deep into the labyrinthine mountains once more. It twists and turns, so much so that one can all too easily become lost in a mass of precipices, under the misleading impression you are continually going in the wrong direction, all the time increasingly convinced that you are penetrating further into the inhospitable hearts of the Taygetus mountain range, rather than heading

---

[1]   To Spanish translators, the noun *decepción* is a false friend: it sounds like *deception* but means *disappointment*.

[2]   Today the journey is considerably less hazardous. The motorway between Athens and Kalamata has now been completed.

down to the gentle shores of the sea at Messenia. It makes no difference how often you have made the journey, every time you are bound to worry whether you are on the wrong track. It is a feeling that persists for the best part of an hour. But if you resist the temptation to perform an about turn and retrace every step thus far taken, reward finally arrives. Finally, after a terrifying bend that takes one along the edge of a vertiginous precipice, the horizon opens and the coastline of Mani appears, where the enchanting village of Kardamili nestles at the foot of the mountains.

Λεβεντειά
(Of gallantry and grace)

"I wouldn't in the least object to having another glass. Would you be so kind, darling?"

He would hold out the glass awaiting a refill, and the ice cubes in it jingled. Elpida had hidden away behind the living room door, from where she would issue half-concealed and conspiratorial gestures. Despite her silent and desperate messages, the situation was hopeless. Paddy's glass had to be filled up again. "Try to drink slowly, that way you can postpone pouring the second – or third – glass...the doctor says you need to serve him smaller quantities." The problem was that whenever Paddy held out his glass for topping up, the only possible option was to obey. Nor was there any chance to substitute good for gold, of replacing full measures of whisky – or gin, or vodka, for he drank all kinds of spirits – with extra tonic or soda water. Paddy would notice immediately, and just as immediately demand rectification. He became irritated, for he couldn't stand to be treated with condescension. Here, as in so many other instances,

Paddy remained invincible. Beneath the outward appearance of a fragile, elderly and amiable old man there persisted a will of iron. No counsel and no warning succeeded in getting him to alter his lifestyle by one iota. And, given that he had survived ninety-six boisterously merry years in this style, one has to conclude that he had right on his side, rather than all those who strive to increase life expectancy by making it boring. (Now Paddy is departed the years do indeed appear all the more tedious).

Many opinions were advanced concerning his supposed fortitude or its opposite. Most people regarded him rather as one might an oak tree; his longevity alone inevitably fed such a perception. Those who had known him longer, sometimes over decades, added that he had never really been all that strong. Even as a young man, Paddy had suffered several major ailments, and he had fallen fell seriously ill during the war. In fact his doctors at the Military Hospital where he spent a number of months were on the point of giving him up as a hopeless case. Mention was made of polio, then of various types of rheumatic fever, possibly precipitated by the harsh conditions he had undergone during his time as an officer in the

Cretan Resistance movement: long night marches, extreme cold, living in caves dripping with humidity, where he had slept little and eaten less. Not only did he survive, but he stubbornly manoeuvred to get himself sent back behind enemy lines, back into his beloved Crete – "my refuge where the Minotaur roars" – and where he resumed living as unhealthily as before. He was a heavy smoker until the age of fifty, and a "monsoon drinker" – the term was of his own description – until the very last night of his life. He ate with relish, and there was little that reached his table that could have qualified as a light meal. He defied every medical statistic in the same way as he ignored every medical opinion, although a fair few had been brought to assist in a diagnosis. With reference to alcohol, it was utterly impossible to throw him off its scent. He could scarcely see, yet he retained an eagle eye for seeking out bottles. If the wine jug used at meal times vanished from its place on the table cloth, or its level dropped more than he reckoned it should, Paddy noticed immediately and, in tones of polite authority demanded the provision of replenishments.

There was a special table that also served as a bar in the sitting room at his house. It was propped up against a wall and its surface had long since disappeared beneath an enormous tray crammed with drinks, along with an ice bucket and a bowl containing slices of lemon. That particular corner of the room exerted a magnetic attraction over Paddy. At one-thirty in the afternoon and at a quarter to eight in the evening, he would head off in its direction without a moment's hesitation. It didn't matter where he had been or what he had been doing there, Paddy set out for the bar with the sure-footedness of a half-blind connoisseur following signposts in Braille. It made one want to laugh out loud to see him planted there beside his arsenal, eyes shining with the pleasure of anticipation and rubbing his hands like a celebrant prepared to bestow liquid blessings.

"Here we are. Here we are. What are we going to drink today, my dear?"

Paddy had the characteristic features of a dynamic vitalist. Every morning he would emerge from his chamber bright and beaming as a bell and fresh as a daisy. He would eat his breakfast, a few hours later his aperitif, then his lunch, pause for afternoon tea, before going back for another aperitif followed by an abundant dinner. He never skipped so much as one of these formal punctuation points to his day: on the contrary he relished each of them, as if every day each pause were entirely unexpected or highly unusual. If in addition there were company, then so much the better. He adored having guests. It was the perfect pretext for long chats and much drinking, as well as stories, poetry recitals, laughter and songs. He also took great pleasure in physical activity. He had once been a tireless walker and a very keen swimmer. He covered many kilometres on a daily basis until well into old age, most of them going steeply uphill (almost inevitably on the way out since he lived at the foot of the mountains). Among his favourite walks was one that ran from his house to Exohori and Agios Nikolaos, where a miniscule chapel was situated on a hilltop with the most magnificent views. That was where he and his wife Joan, together with Bruce Chatwin's wife, interred Chatwin's ashes beneath an olive tree.[3]

---

[3] Paddy could never again recall precisely *which* olive tree. The memorial picnic was, however, extremely well lubricated.

At eighty-plus years, Paddy continued with his daily swims, meaning something rather more serious than a bit of splashing about in the shallows near the shore. Even when he entered his nineties and started using a cane, it was we – his guests – who were at greater risk of missing our footing than he was, for he kept an assortment of sticks and canes along the route, positioned where he could easily find them, on the backs of chairs, hanging on a handrail or propped against the stone chimney breasts... The villagers regarded him as something approaching a god. They were in the habit of murmuring that his will to live was stronger than ever. It was certainly true that he seemed to hang onto life like one of the limpets clinging to the rocks below his terrace. Yet in his desire so to do, Paddy exhibited no sign either of anxiety or of greed. He remained the most delectable company because he was always relaxed and serene. His will to live was like a vital appetite combined with an inexhaustible sense of wonder. Almost a century after his birth, well aware of the line of the dead now gone before him, and despite the vast vacuum left by the departure of Joan, his life's greatest companion, life persisted in continually cultivating his interest. It absorbed and provoked him, granting ever more episodes of euphoria and fits of hilarity.

Paddy's immense sense of humour and minimal sense of his own importance must have been instrumental in this. Ever ironic and distanced, he was only very rarely cutting or wounding. His naivety suggested the malice no worse than that of a rogue or a young rascal.

I retain a very clear memory of the first time the two of us ate alone together in his house. I had come to our appointment in a spirit of respect verging on reverence; it also approached something very close to fear. He was a greatly admired author, in addition to which a venerable elderly gentleman. But every jot of reserve evaporated in the second gin and tonic, for we met in time for aperitifs. We spent the entire meal choking ourselves on yells – he being stone deaf, having left his hearing aids he knew not where – and guffaws. When, before returning to my hotel, I asked him to sign a couple of his books for me, neither of us was in any state to elucidate precisely what day of the month we had now reached. We arrived at a decision through approximation and consensus. He took the first volume, entering his dedication and the date on the flyleaf, before illustrating the month and the year between somewhat wobbly clouds and swallows in full flight. Then Paddy opened the second volume, and stared at the blank frontispiece in comic confusion. "Do you think we are still on the same date?" he enquired. We decided we probably were, and he returned to sketching more clouds and swallows. Finally, he put down his pen, lifted his arms, clicked his fingers, executed a balletic whirl, and launched into singing several verses from an old Parisian vaudeville. The old devil's eyes were flashing fire. In them, one could catch a glimpse of the youthful rascal: a sense of mischief still lurking inside the skin of the old man. Later on I would more frequently witness the same transformation. It was a wonder to behold.

The Greeks have a word for it, and call such an impassioned love of life *leventei*á, endowing it with major significance. *Leventei*á is audacity combined with a taste for wine, women, song – and dance. In the normal course of events, it comes associated with vigour, fieriness, and youthful impulses. But Paddy conserved his *leventei*á until the end of his days.

Τα Βιβλιά
(The Books)

"What are you going to read today?"
It was one of his favourite phrases.
A stock question that he broached every evening,
over the dinnertime hotpot.

Books took up most of the conversation and
were otherwise omnipresent in his house. Over
the table, we would discuss literature, history,
etymology, languages. The dining room was stuffed
with books, and during mealtimes he would often
send me over to consult one to find a particular
piece of information, check the accuracy of some
lines from a poem he was reciting, look up another
he couldn't quite recall. "Now let's see, my dear.
Down at the bottom, on the left and on the shelf
of Spanish poetry, bring me the García Lorca... It's
a tiny bit higher up. Watch out, don't fall..."

The library shelves reached all the way to the
roof, and it went without saying that in order to
reach for the highest books, one needed to stand
on the sofas and then take another step up to perch
on their backs. And wherever there were pieces of

furniture one couldn't climb on, we deployed a set of ancient wooden steps designed for *pukka sahib*. This was an ingenious and prettily carved artefact, originally intended to be used to clamber up onto the back of an elephant. When folded, it took up no more space than a long narrow ironing board, and one could almost open it up single-handedly. Paddy was extremely attached to the thing. He would demonstrate it with pride and his visitors' "oohs" and "aahs" of surprise flattered him as greatly as if he himself had invented it.

His library boasted almost no contemporary authors at all. He was not interested in current fashions nor in future ones, as he candidly affirmed. With rare exceptions, I think he kept the clock turned back from the end of the '70s or '80s, at the absolute latest (we are here talking of the twentieth century; the twenty-first lay in some distant galactic future). By contrast he treasured literary classics and encyclopaedias. And he had an excellent memory on the occasions when it was necessary to know where any one book was stored.

Paddy was always nosing around extraneous subject matter, sniffing out authors who could potentially be included in his wide spectrum of interests. He was a restless and avid reader of poetry, and he would ask me to recite poems in Spanish, or to recommend new names beyond those he already knew from the classics. On one occasion I talked about Miguel Hernández to him, considering that the poet's force of expression and orotund sonority would be a good match for his theatrical tastes. So it was. Our subsequent late nights resounded to the vibrant stanzas of the poet of Orihuela (and Paddy found a particular pleasure in the pronunciation of the Spanish double *rr*).

Paddy was reading, forever reading. Always slowly and laboriously, however, since he had serious problems with his eyesight. "I see you as looking like something out of a Picasso painting. One eye pointing to the east and a mouth way out west," as he put it one day. Even so, he remained strictly disciplined, and spent many hours perusing the book in hand. He sought help from his optician and from numerous contraptions: loops, spectacles of varying gradations, and a patch over his left eye. That the patch was black and sported a skull and two cross-bones was a prank entirely of his own devising. (I suspect I fell definitively into his good books on the day he learnt of my unconditional admiration for Richmal Crompton's William Brown.)

The books were there, always there, objects of affection, almost of worship. Words intoxicated him, to the ultimate degree. He was unstoppable when he began reeling off literary material. He had a propensity for verbal fireworks, rattling off Baroque inventions, always with the brakes off. He was drawn by a thread he was impelled to pursue. When he became exhausted he sought out – or dreamt up – another line of enquiry, more forks in the road that led him along new paths, and so he was able to follow one theme after another, weaving them together without a break. He could orate almost as well as he wrote, and when he was in the mood, he could be the most entertaining and inspiring of performers.

His fertile verbosity was itself the fruit of an effervescent personality, no doubt, but also of his long life. Paddy belonged to a generation happily enamoured of words. The friends both of his youth and his maturity, were for the most part writers or artists who employed words immoderately. One has only to note Katsimbalis, Seferis, Durrell and Miller. They were cultured, literary...and also philhellenic.

The latter characteristic, linked to their knowledge of the land, often also of the language, meant that a fair few of them had ended up working for the Special Operations Executive – in other words, for one of Britain's secret services – during the Second World War. The men operated behind enemy lines, with their base in Cairo, where they met up between one mission and the next. Instead of opting for military barracks, one group chose to stay in an old tumbledown palace that they named Tara, after the fortress of the High Kings of Ireland. The nucleus of those occupying this rickety castle – it goes without saying that Paddy signed up with them at once – constituted a gang of adventurers who lived and breathed the War with wild jubilation. Artists and night owls, diplomats on missions and birds of many hues all congregated there. The place was famous for being the scene of reunions and parties with a tendency to end up in a madcap fashion. All the same, they were fiestas rich in ongoing literary references and verbal acrobatics.

Exactly the same thing took place on their highly dangerous wartime missions. For these special agents carried novels and poetry anthologies in their backpacks. They read them by lantern-light, lending each other whatever they had with them to read, then passionately analysing and arguing about it. An idea lost along the way: that of the cultured, refined warrior. Maybe today, reading some of the texts, diaries and letters of those young men, one could fall for the temptation of describing them as pedants, but in order to be a pedant one has to have pretensions, and such a thing applied neither to Paddy nor to his friends. They were all far too earthy, too human. Whether they had Horace in their rucksacks or not was something to which none of them attached any degree of self-importance.

They all adored words, and the wine that frees up those words. And they adored women, whom they seduced with words: another beautiful idea lost along the way. Words were there to be written down, they encapsulated the most intimate thoughts, dictated their romantic and affective affairs, and they were the thread running through the men's lives.

In addition, Paddy was in love with the melody of language, and was a naturally skilled musician. He spoke impeccable French, prefect Greek and was fully proficient in German, although he always remained modest in that regard. One morning the post brought him an article taken from the *Frankfurter Allgemeine Zeitung*, a review of one of his books that had just appeared in German. Reading it made him prickly. It was true that the critic was very flattering of him. But Paddy believed himself capable of speaking a fair bit of German, and now, having read the review, he learnt that what he had been doing was not speaking German, but rather going about his business "making noises". He acquitted himself well in both Italian and Romanian, and although he had never studied Spanish, when he decided to launch into it – something he did without the least hint of self-consciousness – he did so in the most correct of accents. He had an exceptionally finely attuned ear, and sang unfailingly and perfectly in key. He knew vast quantities of songs and poems by heart, and recited them off the top of his head and with fine oratory. He was also inclined to assert that Spanish seemed to him the most noble of all the Latin languages.

There was virtually no occasion on which he failed to mention – almost invariably in the small hours and after a considerable quantity of wine – García Lorca, in order then to open his arms and offer us a full-length recital of *La guitarra*. He would always pause dramatically when he reached the point of "*se rompen las copas | de la madrugada*" [wine glasses are smashed | at dawn]. As it was among his favourites, he would always repeat the phrase several times over. He delighted in its musicality and the concept of a tragic fiesta it evoked.

From time to time, he gathered words up together, put them into a cocktail shaker, and agitated them. His extravagant and spontaneous translations acquired great fame among his friends and acquaintances. Those who came to his Memorial Service in London (December 2011) were invited to sing two of the verses conceived during nights of wine and extravaganza. John Julius Norwich and Artemis Cooper[4] conducted the choir expertly. The *performance* provided the crowning glory of an emotional and intelligent ceremony, and afforded suitably humorous closure on the occasion of our farewell to the character we all so fondly recalled. It involved certain traditional English songs,

---

[4]   Viscount John Julius Norwich and his daughter. The son and granddaughter, respectively, of his old friend Diana Cooper and both of them historians and authors. He is the specialist on Byzantium. She is one of Paddy's literary executors and his official biographer.

transliterated into a kind of delirious Italian. I here offer you the first verse of one of them, *Widecombe Fair*.

In the English original:

> *Tom Pearce, Tom Pearce, lend me your grey mare,*
> *Sing all along out a long down a long lee.*
> *For I'm going to Widecombe Fair*
> *Wi' Bill Brewer, Jan Stewer*
> *Peter Gurney, Peter Davey,*
> *Daniel Whitton, Harry Hawke,*
> *And old Uncle Tom Cobley and all*
> *Old Uncle Tom Cobley and all.*

Then in Paddy's indescribable version:

> *Tommaso Pearce, Tommaso Pearce,*
> *prestami tua grigia giumenta*
> *Tutti lungo, fuori lungo, giu lungo prato,*
> *perché voglio andare alla fiera di Widecombe,*
> *Con Guillermo Brewer, Giacopo Stewer,*
> *Pietro Gurney, Pietro Dave,*
> *Daniele Whitton, Enrico Hawke.*
> *E il vecchio Zio Tommaso Cobley, e tutti quanti*
> *e il vecchio Zio Tommaso Cobley, e tutti quanti*

It was always wonderful to talk about translating and translations with Paddy. He was interested not only in the numerous translations of his books – he said of one of the French translations that it was so good that no-one would wish to read the original any more – but also in the concept of the work and its philosophy. At different periods of his life he had worked as a translator, and was intrigued by the ins and outs and other intricacies of the job. To his way of seeing, the challenge for every translator consisted in finding the author's "voice" in a language different to that of the original composition. Thus it was less a question of slavishly adhering to a literal word-by-word translation of one sentence after another, but of reinterpreting the whole and giving it a new voice, whether in English or Spanish or Greek or German, from which the same musicality should emerge as there was in the original text. They were splendid and stimulating conversations we had on the subject.

I translated three of his books, and it was always useful to discuss and clarify some of the issues that arose together with him.

Sometimes he would put me through an interrogation, asking about specific details, or particularly difficult passages. We would hold extensive discussions concerning complex sections (ouch, those descriptions of textiles...), or else he would throw down the gauntlet and challenge me with: "Which part of *Roumeli* turned out to be the most difficult to translate?"

At times I cursed Paddy: there were fragments of his writing that required disentangling with such exhaustive laboriousness. Nothing could amuse him more. It enchanted him to see how his writing could put his translators in a tight spot. Sometimes not even he himself could recall what it was he had meant to say, and at those times, he could have died of laughing. He was an extremely playful man.

We would awake surrounded by books, eat between books and sleep beneath books. Books fell in cascades all over the place, and this is no exaggerated or florid term of reference, but a literal description of how things were. When I first started coming to visit Paddy's house, I discovered new arrivals of books scattered across the floor on an almost daily basis. I would rise in the morning and find stacks of books dotted all around me. This phenomenon intrigued me for a number of days, until at last and one night, the mystery was revealed. We were dining *tête à tête* when suddenly there was the noise of a terrible *barrabumbumbum* at the far end of the vast room. There in the distance an entire cataract of books collapsed from one of the tallest book cases. From behind them appeared one of the cats who were wont to patrol the house, and at almost the same moment, there was an aggravated *marramiau*. The enigma was resolved. The cats had been in hot pursuit of mice, or of an insect.

Paddy had removed his hearing aids, just for a change, and remained oblivious. I told him what had just occurred and was advised to: "Go and inspect the damage." I returned to him with the news. All the volumes of *The Life of Samuel Johnson* were on the floor! It proved to be the pretext for further celebratory cheers, for at this table there was never any reason not to cheer. To the Doctor! And to his acolyte, Boswell! .

Literature was at the centre of his life, but did not replace it. Paddy was always greatly distracted by life. This continued to be the case even when he was well into his nineties, making it impossible for me to imagine what he must have been like when he was young and full of energy (and testosterone, something that got him into trouble on more than one occasion: involving skirts followed by fights, sleazy dives and wild behaviour). His work was nourished by life, one long passionate occasion to be swallowed in large gulps, but at the same time there existed a paradoxical incompatibility between his immensely vital appetite and the solitude and concentration necessary to writing. He could be distracted by anything, and we all distracted him too. It could well be that this is one of the keys to the brevity of his output. The other would be the exasperating slowness with which he used to write, and how punctiliously and fastidiously he laboured over it. His jovial and lively appearance was deceptive. Paddy was not a light-weight nor a superficial writer, but much more of an author tortured by his calling. That was the source of the interminable corrections and the hours of suffering spent in search of an adjective or an image. Also of his ongoing dilatoriness, the insufferable delay when it was a question of finally adding the words *The End* to a book.

Whatever the case, given that he never spoke of personal matters, it became impossible to know which came first, the hen or the egg. It was an academic question whether it was that life prevented him from writing more, or whether the enormous difficulty he had in writing made him inclined to seek out distraction and entertainment far from his writing desk. Whether it was one thing or the other, the fact remains that his was a long and productive biography, one that gave rise to an equally rich body of work, albeit a slight one.

When I knew him, he was still immersed in the third and final book of his Constantinople trilogy concerning his legendary journey – from London to Constantinople – undertaken on foot at the age of eighteen. He had spent decades struggling with his old diaries and with a draft version he had sketched out many years in the past. He was working on typewritten manuscripts – not typed by him, of course, for he still persisted in writing in longhand. He went at the speed of a tortoise (or at a snail's pace: a French reviewer gave him the nickname *l'escargot des Carpates*); very slowly, incredibly slowly. Whenever I enquired after his progress he would reply: "I have eighty percent of it ready now". And so it continued month after month...

His biographer and longstanding friend Artemis Cooper asserted that he had run out of steam. Years earlier – many years earlier, in fact

— he had revisited the sites of the last part of this journey, in a vain attempt to refresh his memories and gather inspiration. But everywhere had altered so much, and present day landscapes could not be reconciled with the remembered ones. Nor could the notes taken in his youth manage to transport him back to the high spirits he enjoyed in those days.

It must have been a draining experience to proceed without memories. And without sight...

On his work table he had a willow basket overflowing with spectacles and eye glasses. Not to mention his reference books, encyclopaedias and maps. He was patient and loyal. He used to shut himself up in his study for hours on end, always set hours. But he did not always work. I caught him on a number of occasions reading Dickens, the letters of Robert Byron...and there were occasions when he would appear in my room in the middle of the afternoon. Then there were the nights when he went to bed very late, after having been imbibing with his guests, singing and knocking back the wine with passion. All this at the age of ninety-four, ninety-five and ninety-six.

Perhaps the subject was a source of anguish to him. If that was so, he gave absolutely no sign of it. On the contrary, he preferred to joke about it. He would laughingly say that his publisher had spent half a century waiting for the book, and then correct himself with the gravest irony: well, to be strictly truthful, the person kept waiting was now the publisher's great-grandson...

Paddy used to talk often of literature and of books, but very little of his own writing. And still less of his own successes as a writer. When he was congratulated on them, he would accept compliments with a natural discretion, and with gratitude. He found it praise indeed, and he said so with great modesty. He adored to put on a show at parties: chatting, singing and reciting aloud. Pure theatre, festival fire-crackers, superficial amusements. Whenever he went deep inside himself – and the writing came from these depths – he would become self-effacing, retreat, and disappear. Paddy was that very rare bird indeed: a humble writer.

Kings, queens, and
a couple of duchesses

"Well I do like the idea of a King of Spain."

Paddy made the confession in solemn tones, like someone begging pardon for possessing leanings so lacking in contemporary content. Then he half-closed his eyes and launched into a description of the King of Spain by way of elucidation. A torrent of magnificent phrases was unleashed. He talked of royal ruffs and cuffs and stockings, and of his sword, horse and throne. I warned him that his description was best suited to Philip II at the height of his glory, when he was the legendary enemy of Blighty, according to Paddy's preferred name for his native land. Naturally he protested: he had not intended to describe an overweight *señor* dressed in a suit and tie. He was not in the slightest interested in trashy third-rate kings, but only in those who appeared in their full splendour. It was the *idea* that was so attractive, he insisted. For the same reason – the scene setting, the theatricality – he was fascinated by the rites of the Catholic Church, or what he always preferred to call the Church of Rome, and he himself was given to wearing eye-watering red socks with a blue checked suit. And for the same reason that he had instructed Elpida to serve dinner on an ancient silver dinner service – as invaluable as it was impractical: impossible to cut a thing with those knives – which nobody, other than Paddy himself, could use correctly.

Paddy was an impossible and ingrained romantic, in the most old-fashioned sense of the term. No-one could conceivably describe him as an aesthete. He was too attached to the world of senses – and to the Earth – and too given to irony and self-deprecating humour to be detained by the finer details of aestheticism. And in any case he existed in the midst of merry disorder. Yet he adored set scenes and strived hard to include them in his daily life. None of it had anything to do with formalities, quite the contrary. His *mises-en-scènes* were eccentric and eye-catching. They tended towards the Bohemian and, in any case, once the wine began to flow, things were generally little inclined to follow orthodox rules.

But let us return to what concerns the royal

family, as he himself gave an account of it. One fine day – one of many and only a few years ago – there was a telephone call. It came from a European Embassy in Athens. It still remains unclear whether it was Elpida – his guardian angel and general domestic *factotum*, to whom we shall soon return – who took the message, or if it was Paddy himself who picked up the phone. The issue was that the King and Queen of Sweden were taking a private trip to Greece. They desired to make the author's acquaintance and to visit his home, of which they had heard many marvellous accounts, and finally – to get to the point – wished to know whether it might be possible to enjoy a meal in his company. It was not merely possible, it would be a pleasure taken to the highest degree. Of course there would be sackfuls of food and reams of conversation.

Paddy spent the next week combing through the family tree of the Swedish monarchs way back into the mists of time. When the day of the royal visit arrived, he already knew all there was to know about the royal Bernadottes, and he was particularly proud of having dredged up a number of anecdotes concerning their participation in the French Revolution. So it was the royal pair reached foreign lands and were seated at Paddy's table. Elpida served up the dinner with her customary deliberation and imperturbability – however many kings arrived at the house, she was not to be caught unawares by the least of them – and she knew no restraint in preparing her bombshells of Mediterranean cuisine. Paddy, in his equally habitual manner, indulged in a startling verbal display, employing every one of his battery of charms and anecdotes to dazzle his blue-blooded guests. He talked and talked, of Kungsleden (the "Kings' Trail"), of the Göta Canal (linking Gothenburg with the Baltic), and of the loveliness of Sweden but expounding, above all, on the exploits of the Bernadotte line.

It was nobody's fault that Elpida confused one country with another. Or one lot of kings with the next. At the end of the day, in the eyes of any human being with their feet on the ground – and her feet were most definitely firmly planted – they were all perfectly interchangeable. Nor was it anyone's fault either that Paddy failed to recognise his honoured guests, even though he assumed he must have come across them in photographs at some point in the past. In any case, the problems with his sight scarcely permitted him to recognise even his friends, even when close at hand. Naturally he was somewhat surprised at the complete lack of reaction on the part of his guests when he confronted them with such a glittering display of knowledge, but even he was obliged to admit that kings could be insipid too. As this royal couple appeared, to the ultimate degree, so much so that even their own *pedigree* left them cold. Days went by before someone, a rather better informed neighbour, commented on having seen the crowned heads of Belgium touring the area.

One of Paddy's bosom companions was the Duchess of Devonshire. In England the Duchess is known as a *Dowager* along with a heap of other titles, but at home in Kardamili, she was just Debo, a familiar figure with whom Paddy chatted on the phone. They had come to know each other during the War, when they struck up a friendship that they maintained over decades. They also sustained a correspondence over many a long year, with intermittent breaks, yet always resumed. A few weeks before Paddy died, there was still a sheet of writing paper headed with *Darling Debo* on his work table. Part of the correspondence between these two dinosaurs – she is but a few years younger than he would have been today – has now been published. Reading the book, which is as candid as it is amusing, the reader is at a loss as to what to admire more: his sense of humour or her sense of shamelessness. Paddy's letters are more literary and some of hers are small jewels, but hers bear a terrible charge of malice. Trifling gossip. About whether someone's wife had got together with someone else's husband, and whether he in his turn had fathered an illegitimate child with still someone else, etc etc... The vast majority of those rumours were no more than water long under the bridge, but in Paddy's case they were given an air of gaudy and rabid news stories, for the likes of Evelyn Waugh and Somerset Maugham graced his anecdotes, along with others of similar calibre. And not as distant figures, but presences so real that it seemed as if at any moment they could cross the threshold and come into the house for an evening aperitif.

As to the present...and with regard to Camilla, by now the Duchess of Cornwall, he said she was "very funny", while the Prince of Wales was "very charming". As to Lady Di, the most I could get out of him was that "that person was a rather complicated one". When Paddy referred to someone as "that person" it showed that he was not particularly taken with them, whereas someone he especially liked was referred to as "a dear". Debo never concealed the sympathy she had for the couple composed of Camilla and the Prince of Wales, and certain rumour-mongers recounted that during the period of their clandestine affair the two of them met up on at least one occasion in that part of Greece, where they had rented a well-concealed villa. If that were indeed the case, it seemed highly likely that Paddy had arranged matters for them. There was, of course, no way in which he would discuss the matter. He might be exceedingly dextrous in eliciting information from others, but he was equally so at not revealing any of his own.

"Tell me about the Spanish *grandees.*"

"I don't know a single one of them, Paddy. I barely even get to meet the middling ranks."

"*Is that so?*"

He said this with genuine surprise. As if it were out of the question for him not to come across all the grandees of Spain forming a queue at my front door.

I ransacked my memories of magazines read at the hairdresser's and finally came up with the adventures of the Duchess of Alba, who at around that time was the pet topic, together with her boyfriend (now her husband), on which the gossip press was expending rivers of ink. I explained about her hippy clothes worn with anklets; Ibiza; and a working-class fiancé in the spring of his life (actually the autumn, but she was in the winter of hers, in comparison with which he became relatively spring-like). Suddenly he put one hand behind his ear and requested that I hurry off in search of his hearing aids. This was no simple task: the house is vast and he could have left them anywhere (on a subsequent visit I brought him a tray made of shiny silver plate – blinding to his ailing eyes – on which he could keep them, at least at night. Miraculously, he used it). Such stories caused him to prick up his ears much as hunting dogs do when alerted by the sound of hares. I relayed him all I knew and embellished what I didn't.

I told him the King of Spain had summoned the Duchess to the Palace. After all the Duchess of Alba is such a refined member of the aristocracy, owner of some of the greatest art collections in the country, that once marriage to a plebeian was in the offing, it was not to be countenanced. *Good Lord!* The very thought fascinated him. He frequently returned to the subject in the course of the ensuing days. All at once he turned thoughtful, then he clucked and muttered to himself: "So the Duchess of Alba..."

He enjoyed gossiping about outmoded aristocrats who had come to spend the night, for, in its heyday, the house had received a fair number of them. For the most part they were at least as Bohemian and as much party animals as himself. Now that those of his generation had either died or were too shaky to undertake the journey to such a remote corner of Greece, in his latter years he sought consolation by inviting their children (or grandchildren). He retained links with all his old friends – and their descendants – until the very last instant.

Let no-one be deceived: Paddy was not a *snob*, not even an inverted one. Part of his inexhaustible charm, for which he was adored by everyone – or nearly everyone – was due to the fact that he behaved towards them all alike. This egalitarian way of behaving lay in an exquisite courtesy equally applied to left and right. It formed part of his love of the formal, leavened by eccentricity and humour, and by a lack of affectation which, in reality, is the sole patrimony of those endowed with a genuine intellectual elegance. There was no financial consideration whatsoever in his manner of approaching his fellow human beings. The Duchess of Devonshire was as worthy of his attention as was Elpida, the woman who waited on him. Maybe this was a virtue acquired in Greece at a very early age. And he himself provided a number of leads in that respect...

I had begun to grasp, in the past few weeks, one of the great and uncovenanted delights of Greece; a pre-coming-of-age present in my case: a direct and immediate link, friendly and equal on either side, between human beings, something which melts barriers of hierarchy and background and money and, except for a few tribal and historic feuds, politics and nationality as well... Existence, these glances say, is a torment, an enemy, an adventure and a joke which we are in league

to undergo, outwit, exploit and enjoy on equal terms as
accomplices, fellow-hedonists and fellow-victims.

ROUMELI

Ελπίδα
(Elpida)

...a deep-seated feeling of confidence and of
absolute equality not only with other Greeks,
but the whole human race
ROUMELI

"*E*^{*lllll-pi-daaa!!*}"

There is no exaggeration whatsoever, in my opinion, that in Paddy's last years the one essential person in his life was Elpida.

"*Elllll-pi-daaa!!*"

He would put both hands around his mouth rounding them as if he were making a trumpet. He stretched the length of the first syllable, accelerating and then striking the second, before reverting to a prolonged extension of the ultimate syllable. The voice was firm and sure, but without doubt it was trumpeting. Elpida might have been next to him or some distance away, bustling about in the kitchen or hanging out washing in the downstairs porch. Either way the infallible result was that within minutes she would appear at the trot, a smile on her lips.

Paddy was not prepared to use a bell: the very idea seemed ridiculous to him. The household megaphone functioned perfectly adequately and, for her part, Elpida found that system worked equally as well as any other.

Elpida's father was Mayor of Kardamili at the time when Paddy and Joan arrived to take up residence in the small village. Paddy used to say that the mayor was a man of "high principles". His daughter, more down-to-earth and less given to lyricism, related how, thanks to her father's interventions, the Leigh Fermors became accepted by the locals. Initially this was far from the case, and they were received with mistrust and considerable hostility, as is understandable. What possible interest could a couple of foreigners have in installing themselves in such an isolated village, at that time a place of extreme poverty and backwardness?

There were some turbulent times. A home-made bomb was placed in the boot of their car, and when he and Joan had a small cabin built on the beach that lies at the foot of their home it was, *ipso facto*, blown up with dynamite, a somewhat drastic way of indicating that the beach, whether or not it lay just beneath their home, did not belong to them. Again, according to Elpida, the villagers fantasised and elaborated, taking the pair of them for spies – an insane idea, wholly typical of the inhabitants of Mani, known for their eccentricities and it took her father to convince them of the opposite. So it was that, entirely thanks to the critical intercessions of the Mayor, the couple and their retinue of outrageous artists and friends were tolerated without causing the predicted rivers of blood. The debt of gratitude to the Beloyannis family was never, ever overlooked.

The Leigh Fermors knew Elpida from the time she was a girl, and when she reached the age of twenty or so years, she was invited to come and keep house for them. Joan was a great fan of cookery and kitchens and passed on her skills to Elpida. After Joan died in 2003, the role of kitchen Commander General passed to Elpida. She did not sleep at the house, yet she concerned herself with everything pertaining to it. She arrived first thing in the morning, in time to serve Paddy his breakfast, gave the gardener his instructions, and prepared lunch and dinner for the day. In addition, she took care of all the shopping, and of ministering to the little requirements of an English household. To go no further, the organisation of tea, which involved contacting Rita (Paddy's UK house-keeper), who would then send the requisite tea out to Greece... quite a sophisticated arrangement. At the same time, Elpida also took on the roles of Paddy's driver and personal assistant whenever needed. After serving lunch at noon she would go back to her own home, and then only returned to Paddy's in time to serve his dinner and wish him a good night.

The relationship between Elpida and Paddy was warm and special, one which they would swap back and forth during the course of the day. At times he would carry on treating her like a daughter; at others she was the carer and protector. She was also his eyes and ears. At meal times, she was the person who could discreetly deliver his false teeth to him, or search out his hearing aids among the hundreds of possible hiding places in the house, and who coaxed him into taking his medicines at the necessary times. She took tireless care of his wellbeing, behaving neither like a nurse nor a social worker, for nothing could be further from the case, as her approach was personal, rather than exclusively professional. Her assistance, just like her affection for him, was expressed in a humorous and natural manner, without the slightest fuss and bother. I am persuaded that Paddy was able to end his days with his head held so high thanks to the delicacy and sensitivity of Elpida. She demonstrated such dignity, not only in the commitment to defend his autonomy, but in the exquisite tact she demonstrated in the face of his demands for independence as well.

It also has to be said that Elpida is highly intelligent, equally possessed of a highly developed sense of irony. In her own way, she is as eccentric and unconventional as Paddy. In my mind the two of them are connected, they go together. In a sense they were two of a kind. Both of them were fiercely proud, stubborn, occasionally to the point of absurdity, both possessed of a diabolical inner pride. Maybe this was why they got on so well. Elpida would flee from anything resembling the least sign of condescension. And when, at the end of it all, she considered it unacceptable for Paddy to sleep alone at night in such a vast house, she would sleep there secretly too, without letting him know she was doing so. She'd simply lie down, fully clothed, on one of the spare beds, then feign she had come in at eight in the morning, just as usual. Paddy never learnt of this small but kind-hearted deception.

Elpida it was who brought him to Athens for the first of his operations, and then brought him back home again afterwards. She looked after him during his brief period of convalescence, and then, when his health deteriorated, she accompanied him back to Athens again for a second operation. And Elpida it was who stayed by his side during his last flight back to England, and who unfailingly stayed at his bed until the very end.

Elpida was not in the slightest impressed by Paddy the writer. She had attempted to read *Mani*, the book that told her about her own patch of homeland, but she couldn't get along with it. And her criticism was devastating: "Nothing goes on in it." Then she would add, with perfect aplomb: "It jumps from one thing to the next without rhyme or reason." It was more worthy of note as a further demonstration that her affection and devotion were unconditional, dedicated to the man and not to the famous author. And, on top of all the rest,

her vigils of sleepless night were for the dear old man.

Some months after Paddy's death, Elpida journeyed to England to attend his Memorial Service.

The celebration took place in the Church of St. James, Piccadilly, and was followed by a reception in the Travellers Club. The celebration was not open to the public, and invitations were strictly limited. A large number of those present without doubt belonged to the cream of British society. Elpida circulated among them clothed in the same black dress she wore every day: she appeared immutable, solidly planted on her two statuesque Greek legs.

Neither writers nor academics, nor dukes, lords or ladies, could so much as stir a hair of her head, and she treated them all with utterly equal assurance and familiarity. She had never previously been outside Greece, and had rarely been outside her native village, being almost entirely ignorant even of Athens. Yet there she was, plumb in the middle of St. James's, surrounded by noble and luxurious furnishings, spectacular pictures, and carpets several inches thick. Not a trace of awkwardness about her: Elpida could as well have been in the tavern next door to her home in Kardamili. Paddy himself would have been proud of her.

We spoke to one another by phone on the day when Paddy died. I asked her if *o Kirios Mihalis* had gone well. What I meant, of course, was whether his death had been tranquil and peaceful. "No, not at all. *O Kirios Mihalis* had not been well at all." A note of irritation gave me to understand that my question seemed ridiculous to her. Had *o Kirios Mihalis* been fine he would not now be dead.

That much, of course, was absolutely plain and certain.

Στο σπίτι
(At home)

It was an afternoon around the middle of March 2011. Evenings were still drawing in early and the last stage of the journey had proved as exhausting and intimidating as ever. After all, nowhere is it written that there are easy routes to reach a paradise. Paddy did not live in the village, but his house was only a little further down the hill, standing alone on a jutting platform, which gave it the aspect of a wide balcony suspended over the sea.

The night was black and the track to the house stony and unstable, but Elpida was listening out and came to meet me carrying a lantern. No sooner had I crossed the threshold than she pushed me towards the living room where *o Kirios* awaited me. By this time I was fully familiar with the household routines. The clock had struck half-past-eight, the sacred hour of "drink time". No time for any distractions such as taking a shower or a change of clothes. Paddy's hours for eating and, especially, drinking were as strict as those kept by the monks he so well described in **A Time to Keep Silence.**

Paddy did not hear me come in; he was sitting in his armchair facing the lit hearth. His pirate's eye patch covered his left eye. In one hand he held a glass of whisky and soda, and in the other the book he was reading. He was wearing mustard-hued corduroy trousers, one of his frayed jumpers, and a pair of heavy walking boots. It was the most tender and happy of images.

Walking into that room and feeling the sensation of homely, cosy warmth combined with an artistic ferment was all of a piece. There was nothing original or subjective to it. Anyone who ever frequented the Leigh Fermor home – and there were more than a few – succumbed to its spell.

Let us start by mentioning that the house was devoid of all luxuries, at least in the conventional and contemporary sense of the word: it boasted no central heating; not one window closed as it should, the stuffing in its sofas peeped out of the tattered upholstery; the lights were so old that their shades held up by pure miracle; everything maintained the most precarious equilibrium imaginable (and in the living room there was a forest of drunken lamps all leaning hither and thither). The water came in when it rained, and anything made of wood needed the urgent attention of a carpenter.

As a general rule, nothing in the house was to be repaired or renovated. This had certain advantages, since that way things carried on peaceably enough, everything left more or less to its own quiet devices. One October afternoon I forgot one of my belongings on a sitting room armchair; when I returned the following March it was still there, conserved in dust. There was an overall scruffiness – equal parts British and Greek – and the air of decadence extended throughout. However, the house gave the impression of indelible and eternal harmony and beauty. This was because it was not merely harmonious and beautiful, as it so obviously was. It was by staying there that one learnt that its most profound significance had nothing whatever to do with modern notions of comfort, cleanliness and order. Nothing of the kind. In fact, the house was the manifestation of some of the fundamental values which nourish the highest human qualities; it bore witness to them most eloquently. It was made of light, art and beauty; there was privacy without exclusion, a bounteous conviviality, corners where one could bury oneself in daydreams, reading and contemplation. Nature gentle and wise, taken by the hand, the sparkling Mediterranean Sea surrounding it all. What possible importance could a fraction more or less of blessed Greek dust have when combined in a whole such as this?

The main communal area was the living room, a great wide rectangle, lined throughout with books and divided into three main areas: an Ottoman-style veranda projecting over the sea, lined with benches covered with cushions. The dining room was a vast space with, as its centre piece, a round marble table. And there was an English-style drawing room, with a profusion of sofas and armchairs all gravitating around the chimney piece.

The bedrooms were as simple and clean as monastic cells. Each had whitewashed walls, a strong lamp for reading in bed, and a basic washroom. And books, always more books.

I was put in Joan's former bedroom, something for which I was deeply grateful to Paddy, not only for the trust it implied, but because it was such a wonderful room in which to be and to work. It still contained his wife's own personally chosen library. There were entertaining cookery books, along with novels, memoirs, biographies, some of which included personal dedications. It was a place filled with enchantment, with an ancient and dusty desk on which some of Joan's former belongings still stood. And a log fire which Xristos, the Albanian gardener, carefully lit of a winter's afternoon. This magnificent room had just one small inconvenience: it functioned as a meeting point for all the cats in the neighbourhood. There were than a few of them and, what was worse, they came and went at their pleasure through the cat flap in its door. Perhaps they were still on Joan's trail. She had loved them dearly and it was said that on the day of her death, her room was entirely encircled by the cats.

I think that after her demise, Paddy did not have the heart to expel them from the house. I restricted myself to merely blocking off the cat flap with my suitcase at night.

The whole house was designed in

such a way that inside and outside were deliberately confused, mixing in an indistinguishable manner. Seasonal scents, along with the sky and the wind, sun and rain, travelled the lengths of its corridors and interior rooms. The doors giving onto the garden were as a rule kept open, This was so even in winter, and even when the hearths were lit. One fine day a little goat came into the drawing room, crossed it, scampered up the staircase, trotted the full length of the veranda, entered the kitchen and left the house by the far side, as relaxed as if it were following one of its regular mountain paths.

The kitchen was vast and dilapidated. All the basic domestic electric tools – I don't think that Paddy had the faintest idea of what a dishwasher was – were decades past their use by date. In order to use the stove one had to employ a wedge, since it would not function with the door closed, something that made it necessary to make a complex calculation of estimated cooking times. The fridge was losing water, and opened of its own accord whenever in the mood. "All the electrics have served me well for the past thirty years," Paddy used to say. "Why on earth would we wish to change any of them?" I suspect that none of this had anything to do with saving money but only with prioritising. There were other more interesting expenses to consider, and I am personally convinced that Paddy definitely preferred to give than to receive: "entertain" was a magical word to him. One did not have to be an accountant in order to estimate the outgoings on food and drink necessary to support a domestic economy in true Leigh Fermor style.

The whole house was entirely consistent in not containing a single technological advance or electronic gadget. The phones were a total anachronism; the television phantasmagorical; and the sound system was a portable cassette player coming half-unscrewed. It only further remains to affirm that no-one ever succeeded in convincing Paddy of the advantages of a mobile phone. Whenever we, his friends and guests, showed him our Blackberries or iPads, he would smile and look on with amiable tolerance, as a father surveys his youngest son when he goes crazy over a tinny new toy train set. And he persisted in writing long-hand, using a fountain pen.

In the absence of modern aerodynamic amenities, Paddy enjoyed the luxury of a separate studio: a small summer house. It was a delicious lion's cage, crammed with books, with its own bedroom and bathroom. Just like the main building, it was built of a pretty honey-coloured stone, holed with large windows and doors. Inside there was a further comforting chaos consisting of papers, ink cartridges, telephone numbers scrawled in outsized calligraphy stuck to books and lampshades, encyclopaedias, notes, pieces of biscuit, half-empty cups of tea on Paddy's table and in the surrounding area...

There was an extensive plot of land attached to the house, running downhill to the sea. The part immediately surrounding the buildings was maintained in a more-or-less domesticated manner. A spacious paved terrace protruded over the water, gradually extending to embrace a proliferation of nooks and crannies containing tables and chairs, rosemary bushes and hedges of aromatic plants, stairs running up and down and around, panoramic balconies, carved steles and pebbled mosaics were scattered here and there. Lower down a broad forest spread right down to the same beach, a pristine cove hemmed with some rough steps hacked out of the cliff itself.

In my view it was a highly successful garden. Half wild, half tamed, at just the right point between the two. Joan had undertaken its design, delivering doses of human intervention with wisdom and good taste. It was untidy enough to appear human, and extended the same aura of Romanticism as its owners.

During March, every interstice of the cobbled terrace in front of the studio sprouted crocuses. They were all white ones, with saffron yellow pistils, forming a genuine nuptial array. Paddy could no longer see them, but they had him besieged, nonetheless. One afternoon I described them to him. That was when he informed me how Joan had been the primary gardener there. The bulbs, now reproducing in their thousands, were the offspring of the very first plants she had put there.

That was when I asked Paddy how interested he was in the garden, or in gardening. He stopped speaking and smiled. But my question – I protested – was no piece of nonsense. At the end of the day, so many British gentlemen kept a garden by way of a hobby...did he? He smiled even more broadly. Then his eyes gleamed with mischief.

"No. But I approved it."

Perhaps Paddy needed to accumulate all those initial years of life as a nomad. Also of laughter, parties, and reckless adventures in order later on to be able to infuse his home with his humour, his charisma, and that colourful world he inwardly inhabited. Not to mention Joan, for the home was certainly as much a part of her as of him. What is undeniable is that it took them a great deal of work to create their Eden, where they together established their life at a time when they had already reached their fifties.

Building the house took over three years and, according to Paddy, was both an amusing and absurd exercise. Neither electricity nor a main road reached anywhere near; the workmen understood instructions as they best decided; construction materials arrived on the backs of donkeys; and every obstacle encountered in the normal course of events was magnified in this new environment. Despite everything, the project finally became a reality. And from this point onwards the Leigh Fermors had no desire to stint. The two of them had spent decades going here, there and everywhere, living off the charity of friends, in borrowed houses or spare bedrooms. Now it was their turn to play the hosts, and they became the most splendid pair of hosts imaginable.

Their door was always open. In the course of half a century, there was a constant coming and going of their friends and acquaintances. Joan died, but Paddy stoked the warmth of their hearth and raised aloft the banner of their hospitality. And when he too departed newspapers, magazines, and web pages were filled with notes, memories, homages and compliments arriving from all corners of the planet. Legions of admirers, old friends or passing acquaintances, translators and travellers who movingly and gratefully described their happy moments lived in the Homeric – and Bacchic – paradise of the Leigh Fermors.

The world which Patrick Leigh Fermor regales us with in his books, so often mistakenly titled travelogues, is a fiction. It only ever existed in his mind and in his writing. His home was an integral part of this same imaginary universe.

The house at Kardamili was merged with Paddy's own inner version of Greece. Both were deeply intimate and personal creations; poetic, palpitating, filled with sparks and energy.

When a reader submerges herself in that author's books, she feels like a privileged inhabitant of a world filled with nobility, one that is also gently humorous, elegant and beautiful. To live in his home implied a like experience. It was to inhabit an Elysian dream whose tempo extended into another dimension: a parenthesis of poetry from which any hint of anything sordid or squalid was excluded.

Following Paddy's death, the house and the bulk of its contents were transferred into the hands of the Benaki Foundation.[5] None of this came by way of a surprise: the whole matter had been decided many years earlier. It was the final gift from Joan and Paddy to their *alma mater* Greece.

---

[5]   The Benaki Museum, which is in addition a foundation, enjoys considerable prestige in Greece. Paddy and Joan created the endowment on the advice of their friend, the Greek painter Nikos Ghika, who likewise donated his private art collection to the Foundation.

Φιλοτιμό
(On codes of honour)

...meanness is scorned and almost non-existent; they prize and practise generosity whether or not they can afford it, and the laws of hospitality are as deeply rooted as the most sacred feelings of patriotism or Orthodox pietas...

ROUMELI

Paddy was always generous. It was never a question of a single or a sporadic occasion, still less anything to which he wished to draw attention. Nor did it seem to require any great effort of will on his part. It was something far simpler, consisting in an ingrained attitude with which he approached life in general. He was grateful for whatever gifts life brought to his door, whether in the way of quality conversation, a tasty meal, books, the sun that rose every morning, and the sea roaring at his feet. Life was generous to him and he responded in kind, offering the world his own universe by way of exchange.

The gift was a precious one. Paddy had the rare quality of being able to transform his surroundings in such a way that his ambience assumed a brilliant and luminous enamelled sheen, filled with force and fantasy. The earthly space he occupied was fecund and animated: a cauldron of life.

Friends and acquaintances frequently visited the house, yet Paddy was also endowed with discernment. He had a strong character and knew full well those whom he wanted – or did not want – to have around him. He would reject any form of manipulation, and if he no longer enjoyed the company of someone, he would arrange things so that this was made known, with courtesy but also with clarity.

When people visited, the drawing room radiated dazzlingly, most of all at night. The whole forest of table lamps radiated at drunken angles, and the doors giving onto the garden were opened wide. We were be bathed in moonlight, circled by buzzing insects. On the table shone lines of tarnished silver dishes, cut glass decanters and glasses filled with wine, and old chipped English porcelain plates. The napkins were of linen, and the tablecloth of Indian cotton, a mass of vivid mingled colours. In the midst of all this there blazed a table lamp with its flex of plaited cable and shade of cracked parchment to which moths, mosquitoes and all kinds of flying beetles got stuck in the laborious struggle to scale its sides heavenwards.

His table was fit for an emperor, not to mention the food itself, which was abundant and aromatic, equally full of flavour and presented with stupendously colourful flare. Elpida, whose kitchen was quintessentially Greek and worthy of multiple stars, came and went to the table. From time to time she would take a break and accept a glass of wine. Once the desserts were served, she would wish everyone a good-night and retire to her house, leaving us to continue the party.

We would carry on chatting nineteen-to-the-dozen, reciting aloud, singing and drinking. We drank way too much. At noon we began with white wine, and in the evening, we resumed with the red. Nothing sophisticated about what we drank: it was always wine from the region and drawn from the barrel. Paddy welcomed bottles of wine brought in by his guests from France, Spain or Italy, but the truth is that it was hardly worthy of note for in the blink of an eye they would be drunk in any case. The bottles always seemed to vanish, they evaporated in the sea breezes.

In contrast the large jug set down on the table was a permanent fixture. It would travel as far as the kitchen only to return almost immediately, and would be refilled several times in the course of the evening. It may have been popularly assumed that Paddy could not see, but it was obvious that whenever he reached for his wine glass, he never failed to locate it at once. A rough estimate would not suffice in a matter of such vital importance. I went so far as to comment on it one day, and he clucked back "Indeed, indeed" with a hint of craftiness. He had accurately calculated the distance between the actual space and his poor, distorted line of vision. This, at least, the version he sold me.

Paddy kept company as much with his friends from the village as with the groups of fellow expatriates scattered across the region. His circle of friends was wholly enchanting. They were educated and cultivated individuals, and vivacious company with it. The night watches tended to the hilarious and frequently continued well into the small hours. One unforgettable autumn night comes to mind when, together with his neighbours, Richard and Vanna, we were howling aloud Agustín Lara's boleros at two in the morning. Richard is a British legal expert, who retired with a view to having ample time to enjoy both life and his olive harvest. Vanna is a velvety and beautiful Italian with an incredibly sweet voice and, to add to the evening's delights, a past as a cabaret singer. Yet another of life's gifts: fate could not conceivably have bestowed better neighbours on Paddy, and comings and goings between their two houses were a daily occurrence. Those Mexican boleros were the final act of an all-nighter that had been going on for many hours and through many bottles, one which Paddy had musically initiated when we reached the dessert course with his rendition of an interminable French madrigal. On nights such as these, nobody would retire first to bed, and for all his ninety-something years, he was capable of outlasting us all, however much younger we all were than him.

We would tease him mercilessly over his relationship to the aristocracy, and his relationship to the world of cinema. Few people knew he was the screenwriter on John Huston's *The Roots of Heaven* (1958), and that he went out to Africa to join the crew, living there throughout the filming process. It was a chaotic and disastrous experience that he recounted with a kind of hysterically funny fatalism.

Producer Darryl Zanuck was head-over-heels in love with Juliette Gréco, as lovely and remote as a *princesse lointaine*. Huston was obsessed with hunting elephants, and never showed the slightest interest in his own film. Trevor Howard was drunk the entire time, yet whenever the clapper boards snapped he would suddenly appear miraculously sober. Meanwhile Errol Flynn only lived from one party to the next...[1]

The Roots of Heaven is a weak film, but it has one irresistible attraction: a cameo role for Paddy. Around about half-way through the footage, Paddy emerges for a few seconds. He is highly agitated and shouting: *"They are here, they are coming!"* or something of the kind. The gesture he is making with his arms is unmistakable; even at the age of ninety, he still repeated it each time he wished to emphasise something.

He never once permitted himself to be impressed by the so-called glamour of the cinema.

---

[1]   Clint Eastwood recreated the ambience of the film set in his *White Hunter Black Heart* some years ago (1990).

The atmosphere on the film set reminded him of his school days, and the jokes were rarely better than merely simple-minded (and so it remains: nothing at all has improved since then). Paddy found people in the film world amusing but uncultivated, so of scant real interest. He became royally bored during the filming of *Ill Met by Moonlight* (1957) and ended up fleeing the set, in terror of dying of tedium. Of the entire cast, he got on extremely well only with Dirk Bogarde – the fictitious Major Leigh Fermor. (Of course this is entirely understandable: Bogarde was a highly literate actor.) He also had fond memories of Errol Flynn from the African escapade. One evening, Paddy rose from the table and started to gyrate on the spot. He turned and turned, at the same time opening and shutting his mouth at regular intervals. He challenged us to figure out what he was but no-one could begin to figure it out. He was a lighthouse...in the version created by Errol Flynn! Paddy said of him that he had a fatal tendency to drunken Bacchanalia. What is equally certain, however, is that Paddy's own parties were just as renowned. In one of the letters contained in the published correspondence between Diana

Cooper and Evelyn Waugh, Diana relates how Paddy was admitted to an African hospital suffering from an unusual ailment. During filming with the crew of maniacs, he had got hopelessly drunk and climbed up a tree. He lost his footing, slipped, and landed in the middle of a thicket of prickly brambles (or cacti, since the matter was never fully cleared up).

NOVEMBER 8TH. EVERY YEAR

"Tomorrow it's Mihalis' Day!" he announced enthusiastically.

He was referring to the Feast of the Archangel Michael, his Greek patron, a day on which he opened his house to the whole village, and to any passing friend who wished to join in the occasion.

Paddy's relationship to the archangel could at first sight appear a little bizarre, but it does have an explanation. It refers back to his time as an officer in the Cretan Resistance. It would seem that his name of "Patrick" caused pronunciation problems to his Cretan comrades in arms, such that they always ended up calling him "Petros". This minor contretemps was resolved when they learnt his middle name was "Michael". From that day forward, agent Patrick Leigh Fermor became known as *o Mihalis*.

In fact o *Mihalis* became extremely well-known as a hero of the Isle of Crete.[2] Only a handful of secret agents remained in clandestinity on the island during the German Occupation, and are still remembered with affection and loyalty. Even today, with almost no one now left of his generation, they are objects of worship among the Cretans. The sole mention of their names invokes a tsunami of hospitality and an avalanche of invitations from the descendants of former comrades-in-arms and their relatives. Recently, one of Billy Moss's daughters told me what happened when she and her husband visited the island for the first time in the summer of 2010. As soon as it became known in the hotel who they were, word got out and, shortly afterwards, a

---

[2] Paddy was made an honorary citizen of its capital, Heraklion. He was awarded the honour following his successful kidnapping of General Kreipe, the German Divisional Commander on the island during its wartime Occupation.

line of people coming down from the mountain villages grew and grew, all wishing to come and greet them, or to shake them by the hand. They spent their whole fortnight there going from one invitation to the next, until they were unable to cope. Billy (W. Stanley) Moss had been a huge friend of Paddy's and, like him, a member of the Cretan Resistance movement. In fact Billy had been his second-in-command throughout the operation to kidnap General Kreipe, who took on board the responsibility for the log book. It contained Billy's diary which would later be turned into the book *Ill Met by Moonlight*, and, later on still, into the film of the same title (as previously referred to).

When Paddy and Joan decided to settle in Greece, it was natural for them to consider Crete as their first option. Paddy loved the island, and he was known and respected there. But Cretans are deeply given to festivals and he never could resist a good fiesta. It remains to be said that, had he ever seriously gone to keep close company with the Minotaur, he no doubt would never have written a single line.

So it was that they installed themselves in Mani where, as we have seen, they were none too well received...until at long last the villagers came to understand that their new neighbour, far from being a spy, was a distinguished national hero. That was how he also came to be known as *o Mihalis,* only now with full honours: *O Kirios Mihalis* (Mihalis, *Sir*).

Mihalis Day always began at nine in the morning at the tiny chapel close to the author's home. The day before, women from the village decorated it with palm fronds and garlands of flowers, to beautiful effect. It was positioned about a hundred metres from Paddy's house and, in order to reach it, it was necessary to cross a green meadow dotted with ancient olive trees and flowers of many colours. Down below, in the gaps between the cypress trees, one could see the blue of the sea, winking and twinkling back. The ceremony was comprised of some immensely long chants, vast clouds of incense and a blessing involving giant round loaves of aniseed bread. The chapel consisted in a single whitewashed room. Its interior barely accommodated the priest and his incense burner – the former sporting a cylindrical hat so tall it scraped the ceiling – plus three others. The chapel door stayed open throughout the celebration and those of us who attended took turns to go first inside and then back outside, opening and shutting our umbrellas as we went, according to the changes in weather and the temperamental vagaries of autumn. Paddy only appeared for a short interlude. A chair was brought over for him, and he sat facing the open door, surrounded by friends and swathed in incense.

The ceremony over, the women cut slices off the consecrated bread and shared them among those attending. Then we all descended in a drove to the house. Each guest brought a simple present: old photographs and *aides-mémoires*, or a posy of woodland flowers. Elpida and the other women took over the kitchen like an army of ants, and in no time, more and more trays began to appear, bearing vegetable croquettes, lamb casserole, feta and tomato salad, fried sausages made with red pepper and oregano... From then on the morning picked up speed and passed rapidly, with further entertainment provide by more trays of *mezedes*, wines of many colours, incessant gossip and songs, and children of every size running up and down the garden terraces.

Paddy played the host. He passed from one group to the next, dressed up to the nines, with a blue checked blazer and a folded handkerchief in his side top pocket, not to mention his startling scarlet socks. Women and men always ended up in two separate groups. With the men, Paddy discussed the war and the olive harvest. With the women, he succumbed to allowing himself to be adored, for of course he had always been a *great favourite* among them. His longstanding women friends made affectionate remarks and occasionally even sang serenades. They found any pretext to hug him, or to affectionately place a hand on his knee. There was much genuine affection; more familiarity; and a marvellous naturalness. It was a warm and domestic feast day.

As midday approached, his friends discreetly abandoned us: *o Kirios* must be tired by now, they whispered amongst themselves. Paddy went off to take his siesta, and those most close to him went down to the beach. After a swim we all went back to the house and there we found a renewed *o Mihalis*, as fresh as a daisy. We once again sat ourselves down at the table, this time to attack leftovers from the banquet. Paddy seated Elpida in the place of honour at his right hand. It was a way of showing his gratitude for her efforts, and the success of yet another celebration.

The house was never shut. Day and night, doors and windows remained wide open to all four points of the compass. Anyone could have come in, taken one of the paintings off the wall, helped themselves to any object of art, and be gone from there in perfect tranquillity. Those sleeping within could as well have been murdered at any moment, and no way would we have been aware of what was coming.[3] None of this caused Paddy to lose a moment's sleep. He maintained a supreme trust in all those around him with a stubborn persistence.

"Drink Time!"

Every day, at the pre-ordained hours, he would appear in my room.

Through the cat flap, I could see his boots approaching. This would be followed by a "tap-tap" on the door. It was a polite knocking, but with nothing tentative about it. On the contrary, it was full of happy anticipation. We would then go to the drawing room together. Then we crossed the stone veranda. Beneath us the sea sparkled, glimpsed beyond the olive groves. Or else beneath the moon, caught sight of between the cypress trees. Sometimes he would go so fast that I had to follow at a near-gallop in order to keep up with him. He was not one of those elderly men who drag their feet.

---

[3]   Paddy became deaf with old age. I have been so since childhood. The two of us disconnected ourselves – took out our hearing aids – at night.

Some days he would turn up unexpectedly, in search of company, or just a natter. From time to time he played lazy, and wanted to sit in my room with me. Together we would read aloud from my translations of his books, but only short extracts, enough to justify my presence in the house and his in my room. Neither he nor I had any great desire to work: we preferred to chat. He would nose curiously around my computer. One afternoon, I showed him how Google worked. We typed in his name, and hundreds of thousands of entries came up. Then we entered the names of numerous friends of his. We found them all easily. He was charmed by the invention, even if more as source of gossip than of erudition. A little later, after a couple of whisky-and-sodas, he announced he was going to buy a computer. But his interest in technology did not persist beyond the third glass. He had not yet graduated to using a ballpoint pen, still less a typewriter. A computer? For Paddy?

Paddy gave the impression of leading his life free of fuss or affectation. He accepted the good and the less good as part of the same package. No doubt this was the secret of such a successful existence. We are not speaking here of literary achievements, or of money or fame, but of a personal talent that granted him a harmonious place in the world. He achieved something that was both extraordinary and invaluable: living his life exactly as he had dreamt it in the daydreams of his youth. He had the intelligence, the skill and the astuteness to know how to build on his dreams, so how to live them out. And there was more: he designed them in order to vigorously pursue them to the end of his days.

In one of his books, Paddy says that the light of the Mediterranean exorcised many Greek demons. No doubt it did as much for his. He must have possessed them, just like any other human being – and I actually believe he had a great many – but even so, he never allowed anyone the least glimpse of them. He was a temperate and modest man, filled with consideration for others.

In the course of the Memorial Service held in London for him, one of his old friends read out the famous Biblical passage concerning the lilies of the field and the birds of the air. It was one that could be applied to him many times over. Ever since, at the age of eighteen, he had undertaken his journey on foot to Constantinople, with four books in his pocket, and his mind open to whatever came his way, his attitude to the world was framed. Many years and many experiences came to pass, not all of them good ones. Yet his outlook continued always the same: that of unconditional and devoted surrender to life.

Το παλικάρι
(A valiant man)

... His face was infused with that encompassing smile,
which goes with being toothless at either end of life.
ROUMELI

"I can't see anything!"

He had come to my room first thing in the afternoon, something quite unusual. He was self- controlled, but there was a tinge of anxiety in his voice. He asked me to accompany him to his study and we installed ourselves at his writing desk.

He showed me the text he was correcting. Perhaps the ink in the letters had somehow become smudged? He could scarcely make them out, and he wanted to know whether the problem was with his eyes or with the typescript. He got me to read fragments of writing aloud, over and over again. Then he attempted to read them, but there was no way he could. We rummaged in the basket of spectacles, with him trying on one pair after the next, then again with the black eye patch. No doubt about it, he could not see. I helped him to dial the doctor's phone number, and we waited where we were, quietly seated and well-behaved. We chatted and he fired questions at me about my family, my childhood. His politeness was the same as ever, but he was worried. If he could no longer read, what would be left to him?

The doctor took a couple of hours to arrive. He turned out to be a portly sort of fellow, scarcely more than five foot tall, who emitted loud cries of concern. He resembled the dwarf-sized nun in *Amarcord*, Federico Fellini's film of his childhood. The one who planted herself at the foot of the tree in whose branches the solitary uncle was wailing "*Voglio una donnaaaaa...!*" ("I want a woman...") until she succeeded in ordering him down.

No sooner had the doctor crossed the threshold into the study than he rushed at Paddy and let fly a broadside of furious exclamations. My knowledge of Greek extended far enough to gather that he was reproaching Paddy for the excessive hours he spent reading. He talked on and on, always in the same loud tones of magisterial reprimand. All the while, the two of us remained seated at the writing desk. We resembled nothing more than a couple of school pupils told to sit at the naughty desk: the only thing missing were our dunces' hats. Paddy gazed into infinity without saying a word, and I opted to do likewise, attempting to dissolve into our surroundings. In this I failed. And when the doctor finally tired of berating Paddy, he started on me. Once more, my Greek extended just far enough as deciphering the substance of his recriminations.

As for me, what was I doing just parked there like that? Why wasn't I being of any help under such circumstances? Now let's see, where were *tou Kiriou*'s spectacles, the ones with a little bit of red sticking plaster on the frame and one lens covered up? Well these and only these were the ones he should be wearing at this point in the afternoon, when he had overdone the reading and his senses were ailing what with all those piles of books and papers.

I set to, desperately hunting for the glasses, with his ferocious dressing-down by way of background accompaniment. Indeed Paddy was quite unable to recall where on earth he had put the specs. So when was the last time he had put them on. He couldn't remember that either. Not at all, it was all a blank. They could as well have been anywhere or nowhere.

I ransacked his bedroom, the living room, his bathroom (where he so often read). Nothing. And so a fair amount of time went by until inspiration suddenly struck me, and I stuck my hand into the sports jacket pocket he was wearing. There at long last were the confounded glasses with their telltale sign of red sticking plaster, stuck to the bottom of the lining in the pocket. The doctor quietened down, and I do believe he even regarded me with a new-found degree of respect. Then he started again on Paddy, unleashing still another furious telling off, making a sweeping gesture to embrace every book, paper, the entire final volume of the Constantinople trilogy, the whole library and every last literary attribute that threatened to engulf us. Eventually his lecture ended and he himself departed, leaving the two of us to heave huge sighs of relief.

Paddy was left in a state of melancholia. The doctor's visit, his own absent-mindedness concerning his glasses, had brought the full weight of reality to bear on him. He was feeling his advanced age. All the better then, that what with one thing and another, we were now approaching the magical hour of the evening *drink*. We migrated to the sitting room, poured ourselves each a glass, I regaled him with the tale of the diminutive nun in *Amarcord* and little by little he recovered his spirits. He told me the doctor was a native of Smyrna, from a good family, and in fact a gentle soul. Some years ago he had prescribed Paddy to carry on swimming come what may. But Paddy's problem lay not in swimming itself, but the necessary descent down the vertiginous steps leading from his house to the beach. As he made his way down to the beach, Paddy's heart pacemaker accelerated dangerously, jumping like a little goat.

"It's nothing, nothing at all," argued the doctor. "I'll accompany you, we'll take it slowly, and I'll help you all the way down. Then we can go for a swim together, and I can also help you when we're in the water."

The outcome was that they both put their swimming trunks on and off they went. Once down on the beach, Paddy threw his cane down onto the pebbles and immersed himself in the sea. The doctor did likewise. Once in the water, Paddy rediscovered his aquatic agility, and began heading out into the ocean, as he always had. The doctor followed on behind or at least that's what Paddy thought, until suddenly he heard him yelling like a drowning man.

"*Mihali, Mihali*, for the love of God, come back, come back!"

"What on earth is going on? What's the problem?"

"It's just that I don't know how to swim!"

Paddy was painfully aware of his own decline. He could hardly hear and hardly see. Sometimes his mind, too, was unreliable, and he forgot people and things. All the same, he confronted the sunset of his years with enviable panache.

A daily routine and his insistence on upholding formalities were utterly indispensable to managing his decline with distinguished stoicism. It was therefore vitally important to give proper respect in complying with his everyday habits.

Every morning he emerged from his rooms looking dapper, and every evening he would retire for a few minutes in order to wash and brush up before his drink and dinner. If guests were invited from outside his immediate circle, he would put on a suit and tie. Occasionally he would forget to close the door to his room, and I would catch sight of him sprucing himself up in front of a mirror in which he could probably only make out the fuzziest of shapes. It made no difference to him. He went through the motions in order to maintain his style and autonomy. He combed his hair – he retained a handsome thatch right to the end – and he washed himself before tucking an elegant spotted silk handkerchief into the breast pocket of his jacket.

He always appeared cheerful, and never complained. Nor did he hide behind his years of experience, which gave him more than enough reasons to preach to those younger than himself (almost everyone else). Something he never did. He chose not to mention his ailments or his aches and pains, other than with an occasional ironic aside, and then only in passing. He was the least hard-going or petulant senior citizen you could ever hope to meet.

Paddy was well aware that those who loved him were also keeping an eye on him. He tolerated it, but only provided that no-one either pestered him or in any way threatened his independence. In fact, he teased us about it. I remember an early winter's evening when a mutual friend came to pick me up to go for a walk. The three of us had a drink together, and then she and I got ready to go out. Elpida had as yet not arrived for her late shift, and Paddy told us he was going to his study until dinner time. We wished to accompany him to his door – since he had to go down and then up a number of steps, something that kept us all on edge – but he refused point blank. In the garden we bade farewell with a profusion of kisses, but instead of going out, the friend and I remained quietly crouched down in the twilight, until we saw him enter his lair safe and sound. We followed his silhouette climbing the staircase on tiptoes, walking down the path to his studio in the garden, then crossing the threshold into the building. Now could we depart. We opened the garden gate and at that moment a vibrant and humorously ironic call reached us: "Good night, girls!"

Only rarely did he fall into the temptation of begging pardon for being elderly. Most of the time, he bore his condition with unaffected good humour. Even when his mind occasionally strayed, he resolved matters swiftly and simply. All he needed to do was to laugh at himself, play things down whatever the situation, and in so doing make light of each occasion as it arose. That way he prevented those of us around him from feeling in the least awkward.

One night, sipping whisky at the fireside, he completely forgot who I was. That was when he suddenly and fixedly stared at me with an alarmed expression on his face. "Tell me, my dear, aren't I supposed to be writing something about you? Didn't some magazine editor or other send you out here to me?" I hastened to reassure him in that respect, reminding him that I was his most recent Spanish translator and that, this being the case, things were actually the other way around. Paddy sighed under his breath, and his relief was so comical, even to himself, that it proved well worth another round of drinks...

This was a matter which could be tackled or narrated in a number of different ways, one of which would be melodramatic, even starkly non-literary. Yet where I saw an old, proud and dignified man intent on preserving his independence, no doubt social services would have observed someone urgently in need of their assistance. I also suspected that this might be one of the reasons why Paddy preferred to live out his old age in Greece rather than return to Blighty where his old friends cared deeply for him, and would have been overjoyed to have him there. In Kardamili it was possible for him to grow old in peace and in his own style. No local person would have dreamt for a moment of interfering in his life, giving him advice or assisting him against his will. Certainly his house was no model of cleanliness and order, and while he often wore stained or worn-out clothing, on the other hand he received constant demonstrations of affection, and he was treated with dignity and discretion. In Greece, Paddy could continue being himself: *o Kirios Mihalis, to pallikari.*

It was rare for a week to pass without Paddy inviting someone round, but during those days in the second half of March 2011, we saw no-one. His great friend and neighbour Vanna was suffering from a heavy cold, so she was unable to pay him a visit. On a couple of evenings, he invited other friends round, but each time, at the last minute, he cried off, explaining that he felt a little tired.

These were days of seclusion, intimacy and tender warmth. Elpida, he and I. And, of course, the cats. He was indeed tired, but that would not permit him to alter his routine. At one-thirty *sharp*, then again at eight o'clock in the evening, his sturdy winter boots would appear outside the cat flap, to be followed by his vibrant voice intoning: "Time for a drink!" The evening air was fresh, and Xristos lit the sitting room fire for us. Paddy sat there in his threadbare armchair, with me on the other side of the stone fireplace. Then came the familiar haggling. "There's no vodka in this." "Yes, of course there is." "But there's almost nothing in my glass." "Yes, there is." "No, of course there isn't. Add some more."

On one of those nights he talked long and extensively about his mother. It was a flashback of profound emotion. Another night, we replayed all the names we knew of fishes, in both English and French, and then in their Spanish equivalents. A third night was dedicated to Nabokov...

Towards nine o'clock, Elpida appeared with the dinner: "το φαγητό είναι έτοιμο" ("supper is served"). I was learning Greek, and the two of them were obliging me to practice. I took over in the kitchen for a couple of evenings: one night I made paella, another oven-baked bream. On these occasions, Elpida sat down to dine with us. They spoke a mixture of Greek and English between themselves, in order not to leave me out in the cold. I loved to hear them talk of domestic matters. Theirs were conversations between equals, filled with ingenuity and wit, fluency and tenderness.

The day before I was due to depart, we went to bed early. The following day I needed to be up at dawn to make the hellish crossing of the Peloponnese in order not to miss my plane. We made our farewells that night at his bedroom door. "So soon? So Soon? Couldn't you stay a few more days?" he repeated. We embraced several times. How much I would have liked to accept his invitation and extend my stay – had I not had other commitments, I would have happily become a permanent house guest, a part of his golden dreams – but it was not to be. Instead I went to sleep bathed in his blessings. "Bless you, bless you, my dear." At six-thirty the next morning (the day of my departure), when I came out of the shower, I found him seated on the edge of my bed. He was wearing his navy blue dressing gown made of embroidered satin, and was leaning both hands on the handle of one of his walking canes. He was waiting for me, for he had not wanted me to leave without bidding me a final farewell. At that moment he seemed the sweetest and gentlest man in the world to me.

I raced to put my hearing aids in. Then I sat down beside him. And then we held a splendid dialogue of the deaf.

PADDY: I've been calling you for some time. Didn't you hear me?

YOURS TRULY: I was having a shower and I didn't have my hearing aids in.

PADDY: What did you say?

I repeated myself at the top of my voice. To little avail. The person now without hearing aids was Paddy. We carried on like this for some time, until the comedy of the situation suddenly struck us. Then we paused, holding one another by the hand, laughing like crazy.

I accompanied him to the door into his room, and told him to try and sleep a little longer, at least until Elpida arrived. We said goodbye again, and again he covered me with blessings.

"Bless you, bless you. So soon..."

Five hours later, as I reached the airport, my mobile phone signalled the arrival of a text. The SMS, sent from Elpida's phone, said the following:

THE HOUSE IS EMPTY WITHOUT YOU.

WE MISS YOU.

POLLA FILAKIA, MUCH LOVE.

Time flies, we accumulate too much information, we lose our innocence. We find ourselves obliged to deal with stupidity and treachery, ugliness, greed and violence. And as we grow old, we find that the thorniest part of the process is not wrinkles, nor even physical deterioration, but avoiding the temptation to grow bitter.

Paddy emerged victorious from this twilight trap. In this, as in so many other things, he was an exemplary man. He had survived the war, existing under the harshest of conditions. He witnessed all kinds of atrocity while he was in Crete and Albania. He lost neither his faith in life nor in life's essential fabric as a result. He refused to allow his experience of the world – ample since he had never lived any part of his life as a recluse – to impose on him a conventional way of marking his passage through the world. His own intelligence and lucidity provided something much better.

Prolonging a lifetime of such contentment, generosity, irony and good humour that had already achieved ninety-six, does not happen by chance, but by choice. It must have taken great pains but he succeeded none the less. And from that point of view, one could well declare that Paddy won his battle with time.

Text chosen by Paddy
for his funeral, 16th June 2011

*Now I Joseph was walking, and I walked not. And I
looked up to the air and saw the air in amazement. And I
looked up unto the pole of the heaven and saw it standing
still, and the fowls of the heaven without motion. And I
looked upon the earth and saw a dish set, and workmen
lying by it, and their hands were in the dish: and they that
were chewing chewed not, and they that were lifting the food
lifted it not, and they that put it to their mouth put it not
thereto, but the faces of all of them were looking upward.
And behold there were sheep being driven, and they went
not forward but stood still; and the shepherd lifted his hand
to smite them with his staff, and his hand remained up.
And I looked upon the stream of the river and saw the
mouths of the kids upon the water and they drank not.*

And of a sudden all things moved onward in their course.

FROM THE APOCRYPHAL BOOK OF JAMES,
OR PROTOEVANGELIUM (TRANSLATED FROM
GREEK BY MONTAGUE RHODES JAMES)

Aria chosen by Paddy
for his funeral

Vedrai, carino,

se sei buonino,

Che bel rimedio

ti voglio dar!

È naturale,

non dà disgusto,

E lo speziale

non lo sa far.

È un certo balsamo

Ch'io porto addosso,

Dare tel posso,

Se il vuoi provar.

Saper vorresti

dove mi sta?

Sentilo battere,

toccami qua!

Come, shall I tell thee,

How what befell thee,

Soon can be cured

By my potent charm?

No garden grows it,

Though it aboundeth,

Like furnace glows it,

Yet none 'twill harm,

All guard and cherish it:

Gold cannot buy it,

Say, wilt thou try it

Soft 'tis, and warm.

Has thy wit flown,

Hear, how it throbs within,

lays his hand on her heart

'Tis all thine own,

Ah, 'tis thine only.

"VERDRAI CARINO", FROM MOZART'S
DON GIOVANNI

Τέλος
(The End)

I still managed to speak to him by phone a couple more times. When I returned from Kardamili at the end of March 2011, I called to thank him for the wonderful days I had spent at his house. In April, I rang him again. I had sent him a copy of a book we had been talking about – Nabokov's classes in English literature[6] – and I wanted to know if he had received it. Paddy was just as happy and talkative as ever. But his voice was hoarse, and he mentioned a pharyngitis that seemed to be dragging on far too long. When I called back again, he no longer had any voice left at all.

I followed the progress of his illness via Elpida. I had taught her how to use Skype, so we

---

[6] Nabokov created and taught the undergraduate course at Cornell University in the 1950s. He called it "European Literature of the Nineteenth Century". The *Cornell Daily Sun* called it "Dirty Lit", in reference to the "adulterous novels" it included – *Anna Karenina*, *Madame Bovary* for starters (translator's note).

could at least see one another and chat for extended periods. That was when I learnt that Paddy had managed to emerge alive from a first operation in Athens – a miracle: he was the immortal *Mihalis* again – in May. He asked to be taken back home – "**στο σπίτι** " – at once and seemed to be convalescing reasonably well. But the tumour grew back at unexpected speed. He had to return to Athens, and a tracheotomy was performed on him. After that, nothing more could be done. Family members and close friends began to gather round his hospital bed. There followed a final journey to England. It must have been a terrible journey and he died the following morning. They say he still had time to wash, dress, and eat breakfast. The he took himself back to bed, never to rise again. Elpida maintains he threw in the towel when he realised he would no longer speak again. That would not surprise me in the least. He was an irredeemable talker.

Three months went by before I had the chance to return to Kardamili. Once more I crossed the Peloponnese and its mountains. It was a melancholy journey. This time no-one awaited me, whisky glass in hand. But Richard and Vanna were there, along with Elpida, Maria, Nikos, Brenda, Ken – all friends I had inherited from Paddy.

Once more I took the short cut from the village to the house. It was a fabulous September day, and the cicadas had not yet stilled their whirring reverberations. I found Elpida bustling about in the kitchen. She received me with her customary warmth. The archivists from the Benaki Foundation were due to arrive at noon. Why did I not seize the opportunity to take a turn about the house? She had so much to do, so I would not mind doing so on my own, would I? Another demonstration of Elpida's instinctive sensitivity and tact.

I walked through all the old familiar spaces. They were the same as ever, merely stripped of all meaning. Everything was unusually tidy, and the drinks tray had vanished (at that moment I remember thinking: in whose hands – of which friend or relation? – might such a literary relic have ended up?) The house was still beautiful, but it had now fallen asleep, sedated. Paddy's presence alone had caused it to beat in time with life, vibrate with joy.

Two nights later the place was decorated for a final fiesta. The Benaki Foundation took possession. Paddy's god-children had arrived from Crete, together with Artemis Cooper, the British ambassador, and the entire staff of the Benaki Foundation, not to mention his old friends from the village. At least the drinks tray had returned to its proper place (it was a relief to see it there again, a form of poetic rectification). If the truth be told, it was an elegant and classy party, one that would have greatly pleased *Kirios Mihalis*.

We all dressed ourselves up to the nines, and tables were set out in the garden, laid with white linen table cloths, while whole constellations of lanterns in the shapes of moons, stars and suns were lit and hung from the olive trees. The president of the Foundation gave a speech, a short and sensible lecture that in turn immediately gave way to the musicians, *musikí parakaló* The buffet was more than substantial, despite the fact that Elpida had taken no hand in its confection. The food floated in a golden liquid, olive oil coating mountains of tomatoes, feta cheese, and olives. One table in particular shone splendidly with a mass of bottles. There you could take your discreet pick of any drink at all in any kind of quantity. There was an ongoing frantic hustle and bustle in that corner of the garden, with intense comings and goings that went on well into the dawn. This, *indeed,* is what would have please *o Mihalis* most of all.

At the end of that year, we returned to bid Paddy farewell, this time in London. The scenario could not possibly have been more different. The sky was leaden and heavy, and it was drizzling. The ceremony took place in the Church of St. James, Piccadilly and then we all moved on to the Travellers Club in Pall Mall, for a glass of refreshment. Nothing in the least resembling the Greek fiesta, and the guests could not have been more different. However the same effervescence rose to the surface, a particular legacy of a unique man.

At the church there had been words from his friends, poetry readings, music, along with laughter and songs. At the Travellers Club reception everyone mingled, forming a diverse gathering. I suspect there were numerous lords and ladies, and at least one duke (I recognised Debo's son, the present Duke of Devonshire) plus a good handful of writers. Then of course there was Elpida, and representatives of the Benaki Foundation, various literary translators and admirers, friends and distant relatives. We all circulated and talked amongst ourselves. We were all very different but we all held the same feelings in common, if not for Paddy but in relation to him, given we all liked him immensely.

Melancholy mingled with happiness: sadness at his departure, and joy for having had the privilege of knowing him. And we could all agree on the fact that Paddy's life had been a full and fecund one, copious in its quantities of adventure and amusement. It was not one of those occasions that gave you a desire to add names to a book of complaints.

Yet Paddy's death did bring to an end something else we have cause to lament, something that will transcend his death. He was the last man of his lineage, the last of his kind. With him there vanished an exemplar of universal values that has not been replaced by another of equivalent worth.

He incarnated attributes which are no longer fashionable. We live in times where composure, valour and stoicism are devoid of all meaning. We inhabit a weak and flabby society, overlaid with sentimentality, one that has made individual exhibitionism its flag of modernity. A society in which the slightest setback or frustration requires the assistance of an army of psychologists, along with innumerable and ridiculous therapies, obsessively centred on what one is or feels; on what one has been, will be, and either wills to be or not to be... In the midst of this circus of insensitivity, egotism and self-absorption, Paddy's humorous self-restraint, his consideration for others, his courage and his extreme modesty, were models of mental graciousness and emotional *savoir-faire*.

Printed on the last page of the pamphlet we were handed for the Memorial Service in Piccadilly was Paddy's own choice of words. They are addressed to his friends, but they define him to perfection. They neatly express who he was, his human quality, his generosity and – most of all – the role he had accorded himself in life:

Love to all and kindness to all friends,
and thank you all for a life of great happiness.
PATRICK LEIGH FERMOR

Biographical Appendix

Patrick Leigh Fermor was born in 1915. His father was an eminent British geologist posted to India, shortly to be followed out there by his mother. They left Paddy behind, a practice that was fairly common for sons of imperial civil servants. He spent the first years of his life in the north of England, in the care of a kindly farming family, from whose lips he never heard either an order or a reprimand. It was a happy and untrammelled childhood, and when his mother and his sister came to collect him he referred to them as the "two beautiful foreigners" from whom he fled at full speed.

He had grown into a lively and unruly youth, ever curious, one with a huge appetite for learning, but ill-suited to conventional schools. Having attended any number of them and suffered expulsion from the last — according to him, after being caught holding hands with the daughter of the village greengrocer — his family considered it might be preferable to pack him off on track to a military career. They sent him off to London where – as was only to be anticipated – he at once discovered kindred spirits in Bohemian circles. As might further have been expected, the putative military career vanished into thin air. Paddy was absolutely clear that he was not going to get put under any discipline other than one he chose himself. His vocation had to be to teach himself everything. And from childhood onwards he had been a precocious reader, with a genuine passion for foreign languages, history and poetry.

In December 1933, at the age of eighteen, he had an early but dramatic rethink, the result – it would seem – of a violent hangover. He was sick of parties and felt empty, lacking all sense of the future. He dreamt of escaping from England, reaching some distant and exotic land, where he could return to zero and start writing. That was when he took the decision that would change his life, to walk to Constantinople.

Dressed in a leather jacket and weighed down only with a change of clothes, a volume of Horace and a book of poems, together with his sleeping bag, notebooks, and a metal cylinder full of pencils, he embarked for the Hook of Holland, the point of departure for his trip across Europe. Ahead of him lay the raw cold of winter, to be endured with only the small amount of money he had managed to pull together, in addition to a family allowance amounting to no more than £4 a month. Altogether, just about enough for him to remain precariously alive. He resolved his financial dearth by sleeping in people's spare rooms, country houses or log huts, à la belle étoile. Or by putting himself at the mercy of hospitable souls he met along the way. He was almost invariably received with affection, when not with actual enthusiasm. He was young, avid for knowledge, very good looking; he had charisma in spades and an exceptional talent for conversation. All were qualities he retained in adult life and which came in immensely useful in his vagabond years. All who came across him in this early period are unanimous: he was a perfect "*charmeur*" and that was how he was always received.

Little by little Paddy set about weaving a network of friends and protectors. They in turn would provide him with letters of introduction to other potential friends and protectors, to whom he could turn at later stages of the journey. The strategy was so successful that, nearing the end of his project, Paddy was afforded accommodation in a fair few mansions, even in palaces. He moved on unhurriedly, for he might choose to stay in the same place a few days, a whole week, or even up to a month. His itinerary was also open to any enticing diversions, any unexpected fork in the road.

He finally set foot in Constantinople on New Year's Day, 1935, just as he was turning twenty years old. He had shared the table of peasants, shepherds, merchants and aristocrats. He had slept in huts, monasteries, castles or under trees. His luggage, already light on departure, had diminished still further until it was stripped of everything apart from his pencils and notebooks. But his extraordinary pilgrimage proved to be the best form of education there was, no doubt uniquely suited to a temperament such as his. The Europe he left behind was destined to be on the point of vanishing, swallowed up in the roar of the Second World War, and the lessons he learnt on its highways were definitive in his formation. They sowed in him the seeds of his future life as a writer, and made of him the ideal traveller. By turns Stoic and Franciscan as circumstances dictated, he was also a sensual Sybarite when the occasion arose.

From Turkey, Paddy continued on to Greece. The encounter with the Hellenic and Byzantine world so stirred and shocked him that it led to a lasting, profound and dynamic love for the region. He learnt Greek and travelled the length and breadth of the country. In Athens he met the Romanian Princess Balasa Cantacuzène, twelve years older than himself and who had only just separated from her husband, a Spanish diplomat. The *coup de foudre* was mutual, and they fell into each other's arms, moved into an old mill and for some considerable period lived the Arcadian dream. They loved and she painted while he attempted to write. At Balasa's suggestion, they moved to Moldavia, in the north of Romania, to live in her historic family mansion, inherited by herself together with her sister Elena. They managed to prolong their dreamlike idyll another few years in their new surroundings and it was a golden epoch for the two of them.

Baleni, surrounded by rural villages and farmed fields, was a declining, charming mansion of great antiquity. The two Cantacuzène sisters, aristocrats fallen on hard times, were endowed with all the Graces. They were beautiful, brave, eccentric, amusing and – above all – cultured. Perhaps there was no longer any money in the family, but their home was still filled with books, paint-brushes, and musical scores. Days flowed by, rich in events, conviviality and romance. There were continual excursions throughout the region, all-night parties, concerts, poetry readings, moonlit walks, with occasional escapades back to Paddy's native land of Blighty.

The war put paid to this bucolic and idyllic lifestyle. Paddy at once went back to London to join up. When he departed Moldavia, he bade Balasa and Helena farewell, convinced that he would be back within a few months. He was not to see them again for more than twenty-five years, when at long last he picked up their trail behind the Iron Curtain. *Baleni* had been impounded and the two sisters were reduced to living in penury in an attic in Bucharest, giving lessons in English, French and painting. In 1965, he finally obtained a visa to go to Rumania, and spent a few clandestine days in their company, for the Ceausescu regime forbade providing accommodation to foreigners. He found them poorer than ever, but with exactly the same charm and sense of humour they had enjoyed in the days of their glorious youth. The friendship between the three of them remained just as close, until the death of the two sisters.

On learning that Paddy spoke Greek, the Intelligence Services recruited him at the earliest opportunity. In 1940 he was made the official British go-between for the Greek army at that time fighting the Italians in Albania. When Greece fell, Paddy's unit was transferred to Crete, and when the island also fell, he stayed on for another eighteen months, living in caves hidden deep in the mountains. He passed himself off as a shepherd, but his mission was to co-ordinate the factions of the legendary Cretan Resistance.

Following Italy's surrender, Paddy spent a short time in Cairo before being again sent back to Crete, this time by parachute, and with one particular objective: to organise a commando to kidnap General Kreipe, commander of the German Division based on the island. The operation was planned and executed with great brilliance, imagination and risk. Paddy and his unit seized the general from under the nose of enemy troops. Over the following days they had to keep on the move in order not to have their location pinpointed. The general was accorded every kind of respect due his rank, but was not spared long forced marches over the craggy peaks of the island.

This chapter of history, of itself intrinsically novelesque, was consecrated with the ultimate literary blessing. It so happened that one morning, as dawn broke, the prisoner gazed out over the magnificent landscape that lay at his feet and murmured: "*Vides ut alta stet nive candidum | Socrate...*" The future writer, who sat smoking a cigarette beside him, continued: "*Nec iam sustineant onus | Silvae laborantes, geluque | Flumina constiterint acuto*".[7] They are the first verses of one of Horace's Odes and, as it happened, one of the few Paddy had learnt by heart (or so he vowed).

The kidnapping of the general passed into the annals of Cretan history and Leigh Fermor was acclaimed a hero. Even during the War, in October 1943, he was awarded the Order of the British Empire. The Greek government made

---

[7]   You see how [Mount] Soracte stands out white | with deep snow, and the struggling trees can | no longer sustain the burden, and the rivers | are frozen with sharp ice.

(From Horace's *Odes*, 1.9)

him an Honorary Citizen of Heraklion, and the British awarded him the Distinguished Service Order.[8] Paddy turned down a knighthood in 1991, but accepted in 2004, and was actually knighted in February, coincidentally on the occasion of his eighty-ninth birthday. W. Stanley Moss (Billy), Paddy's second-in-command throughout this adventure, had kept a diary that was published at the end of the war under the title *Ill Met by Moonlight.* The book enjoyed great success, and transferred to the big screen under the same title, directed by Michael Powell and produced by Emeric Pressburger, in 1957.

Once the war was over, Leigh Fermor undertook a six-month-long journey through the Antilles. He was accompanied throughout by Joan Rayner (née the Honourable Eyres Monsell), a photographer he had come to know in Cairo. Joan was a native of Worcestershire. The daughter of a Viscount and Conservative peer she had received

---

[8]   Paddy turned down a knighthood in 1991, but accepted in 2004, and was actually knighted in February, coincidentally on the occasion of his eighty-ninth birthday.

something of an *ad hoc* education – meaning little or none, as she herself explained – but she had always opted to take unconventional paths and, above all, keep unconventional company. She was beautiful, elegant and appeared delicate. The delicacy was deceptive, however: no fragile or prim and proper woman could possibly have travelled under the conditions she survived. Keen on both photography and architecture, her images were used to illustrate a number of books by Leigh Fermor, among others.

Joan adored cats in general and Greek cats in particular. They came in and out of the Leigh Fermor house in Greece in droves, and it was said that at least eight of them kept Joan company in her final hours. She died in June 2003, at the age of ninety-one, having been the writer's wife and companion for over fifty years. The friends who provided her obituaries described her as devoted, loyal, amusing and generous, but who preferred to keep to the shadows than to bathe in the characteristic brilliance of her environment.

Their adventures in the Antilles bore fruit in Patrick Leigh Fermor's first book, *The Traveller's Tree*, which was published in 1950.

There followed years of round tours and distant destinations. Leigh Fermor and his wife were notably independent migrating birds who frequently voyaged in different directions, while always maintaining an ongoing contact and dialogue. Fragments of Joan's love letters were later adapted for publication by Paddy himself (*A Time of Gifts* in 1977; *Three Letters from the Andes* in 1991).

The couple pursued their nomadic lifestyle during the 1960s and '70s. Both must have been endowed with enviable physical strength, and a considerable ability to adapt. Many of their expeditions took place under the most Spartan conditions; they would walk for hours and sometimes days under a relentlessly blazing sun or lashed by sheeting rain, frequently sleeping out in the open air, often eating either badly or hardly at all. But it is also the case that on other occasions they were received in the most luxurious of castles and palaces. Flexibility seems to have been an inherent trait in both the Leigh Fermors. One could come across them tranquilly installed wherever they were, always with the same equanimity, whether in an abandoned and rat-infested castle; in the attic of an old pub; on the flamboyant yacht of a millionaire;

a cheap Bed and Breakfast; an army tent erected in the midst of a desert waste; a shepherd's hut or in one of the luxurious four-poster beds of the Duchess of Devonshire.

They journeyed to all four points of the compass, yet always stopped off in Greece, the country the two of them adored. *Mani* (1958) and *Roumeli* (1966) are splendid texts, inspired by their innumerable travels the length and breadth up and down their beloved *Ellada*.

In a letter dated sometime in August 1962, Leigh Fermor describes with emotion and in great detail the place to which he would remain attached for the rest of his life. In one of his innumerable excursions through the Peloponnese, he and Joan had discovered a tiny, wild and remote plot of land on a small peninsula covered with olive trees, descending to the sea in terraces punctuated by tall cypresses. There they pitched their army tent and there they built their new house up around it over the years which followed. There was no water or electricity, not even a road, but over time they transformed the place into a sacred hearth to which friends and admirers flocked in (principally to imbibe the white wine of the region).

Seated in his house, in his own study surrounded by books and encyclopaedias, Paddy at long last found the necessary space and stability in which to give some order to the already legendary exercise books, filled with notes on his first journey to Constantinople. The long and detailed process that followed gave rise to two works, *A Time for Gifts* (1977) and *Between the Woods and the Water* (1986) which attracted a cult following. All his books sold very well, and once he reached his sixtieth year, Patrick Leigh Fermor became not only a well-known author, but a popular public figure, drawing a considerable cult following.

In the years which followed Paddy tried in vain to complete what should have been the final volume in his Constantinople trilogy. At the same time, he and Joan continued to travel and to receive guests from all over the world. They lived in Greece, but made regular visits to England, where Joan had inherited a country house that passed to him on her death.

Paddy died in that house, in Worcestershire on 10th June 2011. He is buried next to Joan in the village parish churchyard.

CPSIA information can be obtained
at www.ICGtesting.com
Printed in the USA
LVOW03s1752210318
570659LV00003B/684/P